GW00357422

Recovering The Past

Recovering The Past is dedicated to the personnel of DOVO-SEDEE for their continual efforts in making a once shattered land safe again for all, and to the men of the Australian Imperial Force who gave so much.

Recovering The Past

IAN ALDERMAN

UNIFORM

First published by Uniform
an imprint of the Unicorn Publishing Group LLP, 2017
Revised 2018

5 Newburgh Street
London W1F 7RG

www.unicornpublishing.org

All rights reserved. No part of this publication may be reproduced, stored
in or introduced into a retrieval system, or transmitted, in any form or by
any means (electronic, mechanical, photocopying, recording or otherwise),
without the prior written permission of the copyright holder and the
above publisher of this book. The publisher has made every effort to
contact the current copyright holders to the pictures included in this book.
Any omission is unintentional, and the details should be addressed to the
Unicorn Publishing Group to be rectified in any reprint.

© 2017, 2018 Ian Alderman

ISBN 978-1-910500-82-8

Printed and bound by Gomer Press, Wales

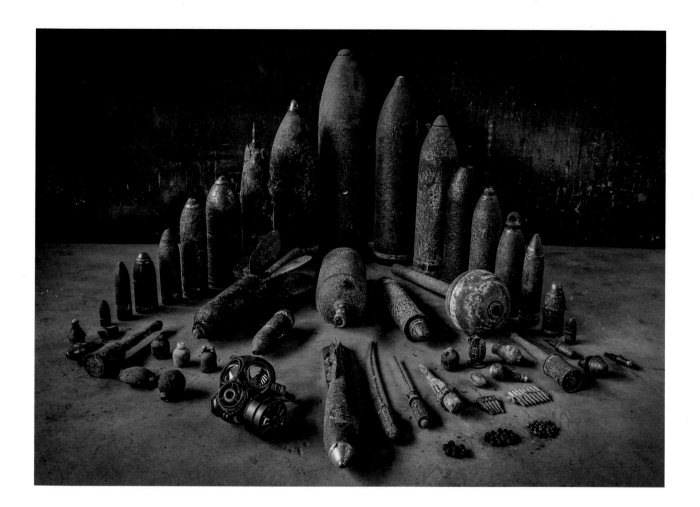

Recovering The Past – Introduction

Recovering The Past is an innovative photographic project which portrays a journey of human dedication of two distinct parties with origins a century apart, yet who are united through a disastrous conflict. The project's twenty-five thought-provoking images are a compelling visual exploration of post-conflict achievement and reconciliation, whose narrative examines the consequences and legacies of human conflict that persist long after the guns fall silent.

Photographer Ian Alderman has combined artistic inspiration gleaned from the work of Australian artistic and cultural icons Frank Hurley and Will Longstaff, by using modern digital manipulation techniques to montage images of 'Australian Imperial Force' (AIF) personnel into his own photographs of the operations of the Belgian Defence bomb disposal unit, DOVO-SEDEE.

A century on from the battles of the Great War, the former Ypres Salient now plays host to an ongoing military operation that routinely engages with a lethal legacy of that conflict, that of unexploded ammunition.

The Poelkapelle based bomb disposal company has been operating since 1920. Initially it was expected that the clear-up would be completed within three years, this was not to be the case.

Today, a century after the signing of the Armistice, DOVO-SEDEE's distinctly marked vehicles will depart its Poelkapelle barracks to collect the continually unearthed ammunition from the fields, construction sites and gardens of Flanders, all once the former battlefields of the Great War. In 2017 alone, DOVO-SEDEE's Poelkapelle team recovered 220 tonnes of ammunition from in and around the former Ypres Salient. With its striking portrayal of men of the AIF, *Recovering The Past* plays an important role in giving back individual identity to those who fought in the Great War. The faces of the 'diggers' who gaze out from this project's images reveal proud men whose identity war inevitably turned to military terminology or at worse a statistic.

Through compressing a century of time, the images suggest a team effort now exists. The diggers depicted have a new and important role in a new world that they selflessly helped create. The human and social trauma inflicted on Australian post-war society extended far beyond that suffered by its soldiers fighting at the front. The thousands of traumatised returning servicemen, and the suffering of the widows and orphans of those men who perished are each a consequence of the Great War.

Unexploded ammunition and conflict-induced trauma are not unique to the Great War. All conflicts since and those to come will leave a comparable tangible legacy for future generations to deal with. In raising the profile of these consequences of human conflict, *Recovering The Past* conveys a universal message with timeless relevance. All five divisions of the AIF saw action in the Third Battle of Ypres or Passchendaele. Despite suffering 38,000 casualties in a period of just eight weeks of fighting, the AIF made a significant contribution to the successful outcome of the fighting in Flanders.

Recovering The Past does not give the Australian men depicted in the photographs a voice, but it does give them a presence and a forum in which to be seen. They will once again stand tall to the viewers of this project.

Ian Alderman, London, 2018

Frank Hurley

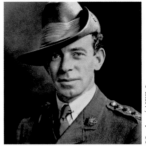

Hurley/AWM

Australia's contribution to the history of the Great War as we know it is not limited to the fighting. Much of what happened in the trenches was revealed to us through the powerful photographs and montages created by Captain James Francis (Frank) Hurley.

Taking great personal risks to capture a true picture of battle, his photographs graphically portray the daily existence of the fighting man in the shattered and torturous landscape of the Ypres Salient. Hurley's commitment to create battlefield scenes from multiple negatives brought him into regular conflict with official historian Charles Bean.

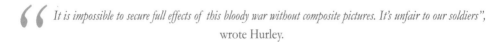

It is impossible to secure full effects of this bloody war without composite pictures. It's unfair to our soldiers",
wrote Hurley.

His famed and celebrated composite images were an essential inspiration behind the concept of *Recovering The Past*. Several of Hurley's photographs of the Great War feature within the images of this project.

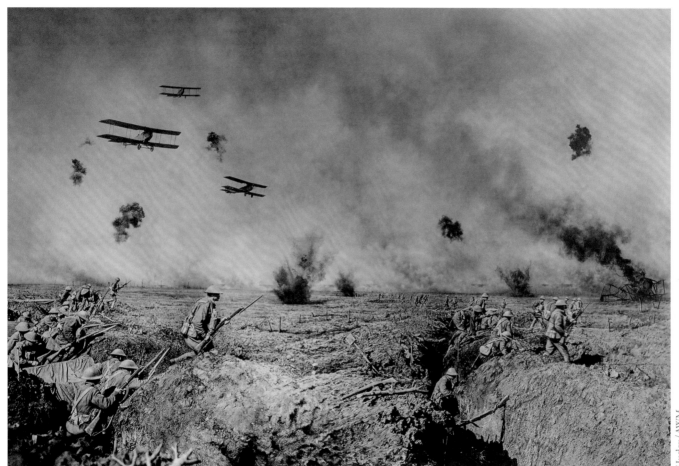

Hurley/AWM

Menin Gate at Midnight
by Will Longstaff

The celebrated painting *Menin Gate at Midnight* was created by Australian artist Will Longstaff in 1927.

Longstaff's artistic approach to depicting personnel in his painting is adopted and used to great effect in *Recovering The Past*. The transparent appearance applied to the Australian personnel in this project has imbued them with a sense of peace, greatly at odds with the war-torn environment in which they fought.

Menin Gate at Midnight commemorates those soldiers with 'no known grave' on the Western Front. Longstaff produced this most poignant of paintings after attending the dedication ceremony of the Menin Gate itself.

Touring Australia between 1928–1929, *Menin Gate at Midnight* was to be seen by record crowds.

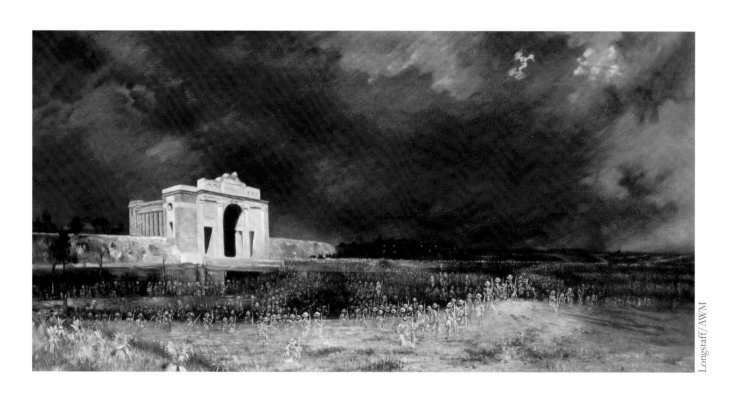

Longstaff / AWM

Recovered toxic ordnance is handled and dismantled by personnel wearing full biochemical protection suits. Although the gas shells are now a century old their contents have lost none of their toxicity.

The shell, with its toxic and explosive content, is destroyed under highly controlled conditions. Depending on the shell's contents, this is done by detonation or burning in specific dismantling facilities. The off-gases are treated prior to release into the open air. Scrap and debris following the destruction of the projectiles are dealt with by specific contractors.

The Australian soldiers in this image are all carrying box respirators, essential for survival in trench warfare.

On 22 April 1915 and just 8km from DOVO-SEDEE's Poelkapelle barracks, the Germans released 168 tons of Chlorine gas from 5,730 cylinders buried in their front line trenches towards positions held by French colonial troops.

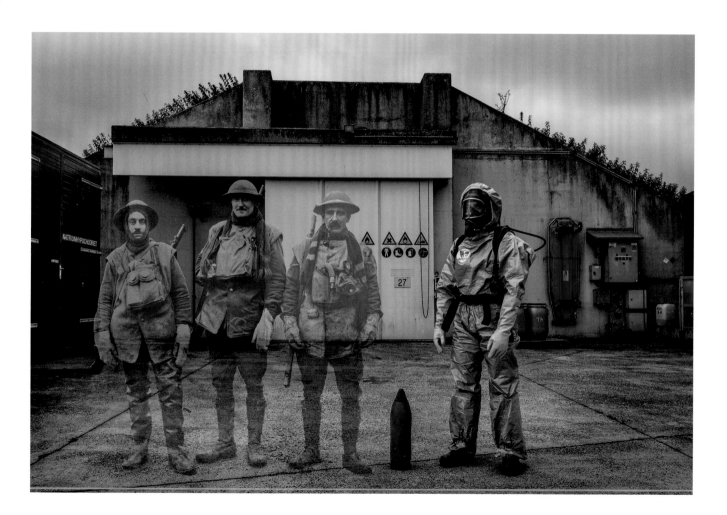

The construction of new buildings or road developments carries a particularly high risk to building contractors. Construction sites in Flanders will occasionally employ civilian contracted detection companies to identify and manage the inevitable unearthing of unexploded ammunition until its recovery by personnel of DOVO-SEDEE.

The construction site in this image is in Ypres. Nine Victoria Crosses were awarded to the men of the AIF for their gallantry in the battles that raged around this town in 1917.

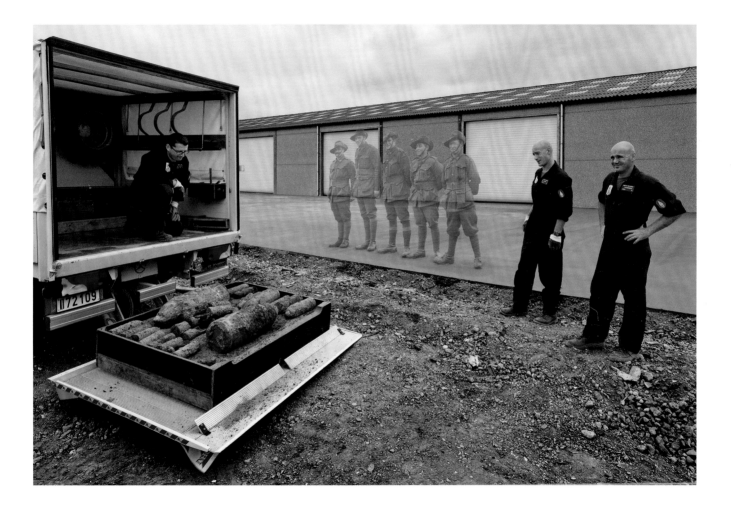

Crate number 143 of Great War vintage ammunition recovered from Flanders' former battlefields awaits its destruction; it is a sobering indication of the scale of the problem.

Each shell is barcoded primarily for the purpose of traceability through the complex disposal process. Another advantage of this system is that it allows the creation of a database of all types of ammunition recovered on the battlefield. The chalk circle indicates the filling point of the shell's chemical contents during its manufacture. The grooving to the band on each shell's base indicates it has been fired.

The Third Battle of Ypres or 'Passchendaele' was comprised of a series of localised battles. In September 1917, and in just over a week's fighting during the 'Battle for Menin Road' and at 'Polygon Wood', the AIF sustained almost 11,000 casualties.

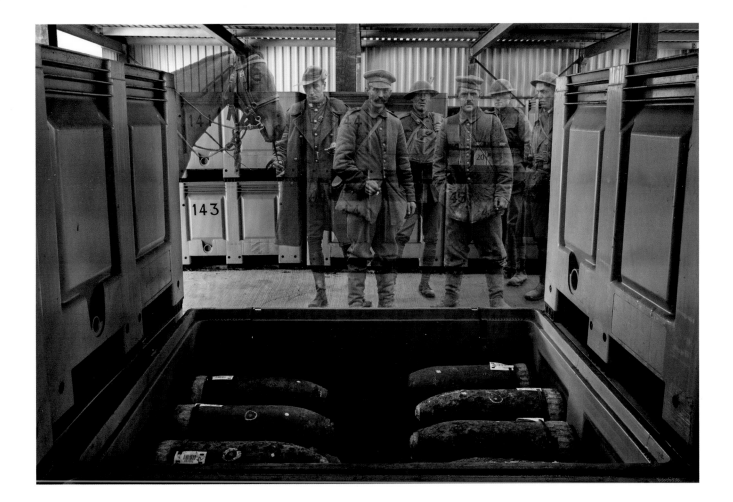

Every item of recovered ammunition that cannot be immediately identified as non-toxic is X-rayed for further examination. Gas or 'toxic' shells (such as Mustard or Phosgene gas munitions) will be identified in the X-ray as showing fluid-based contents. A 'neutron-induced gamma ray spectrometer' will then identify the precise chemical compound before the appropriate disposal can begin.

Immediately prior to being dismantled – in a now obsolete process – recovered Phosgene gas shells were cooled in large refrigerators to lower the gas content below its natural boiling point of 7 degrees centigrade.

In October 1917, twenty men of the AIF were the first to reach the ruins of Passchendaele Church. Completely isolated and unsupported they were forced to withdraw to their own lines.

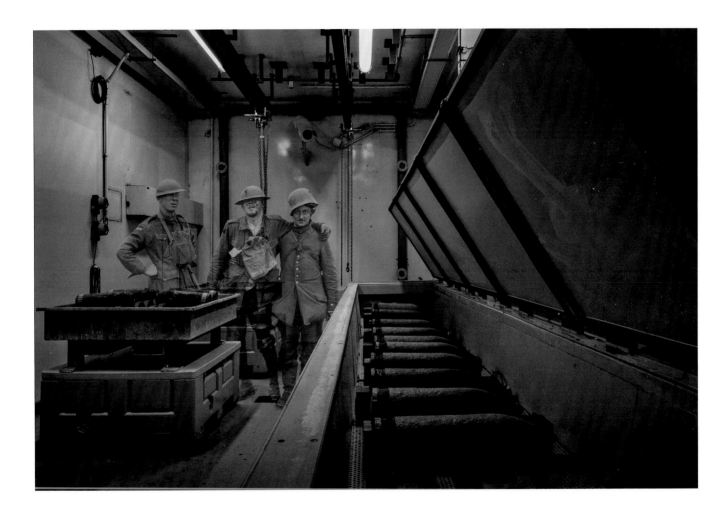

Farming practices in this seemingly innocuous landscape have unearthed this 8in British High-explosive shell weighing 90kg. This particular shell is termed a 'dud', a shell that was fired but failed to explode.

Designed by the architect Sir Reginald Blomfield and unveiled on 24 July 1927, the Menin Gate is a memorial to the British and Empire soldiers killed in the Ypres Salient up until 15 August 1917 and whose graves are unknown. It is inscribed with 54,896 names, 6,198 of which are Australian.

The names of the 34,949 British and New Zealand men missing after this date are inscribed on the Tyne Cot Memorial to the Missing instead.

A record at the Australian War Memorial provides a reminder of the impact on Australian families of the struggle in the Ypres Salient. This index of the Australian names on the gate was compiled most likely in 1927 or 1928. The index reveals that virtually every community across Australia at that time had at least one soldier 'laying where he fell' in the Ypres Salient.

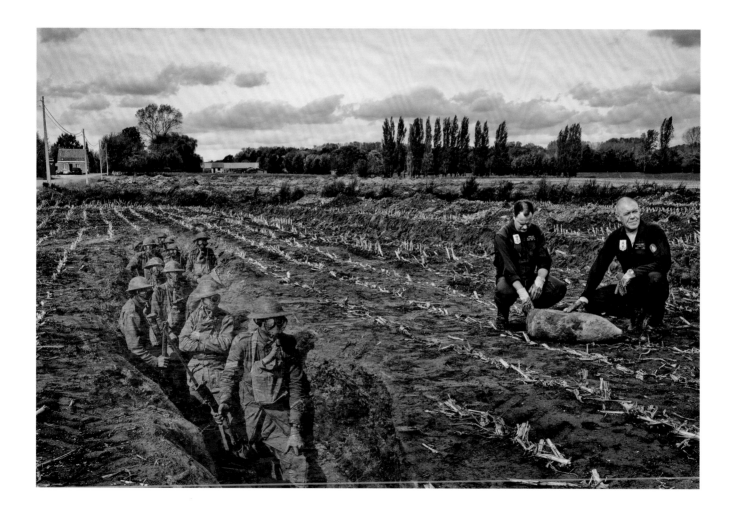

During the period 1975–1978, 665 tonnes of High-explosive shells and 105 tonnes of gas shells were collected; the combined figure for 1983–1986 was 860 tonnes. In 2004, at a site near Ypres, a single stockpile of 3,000 German shells was unearthed.

In 2015, DOVO-SEDEE's Poelkapelle barracks collected 173.4 tonnes of ammunition comprising 8,690 projectiles of which 1,018 were of toxic contents. In 2016, the same team responded to 2,267 calls from which 197.7 tonnes of ammunition were recovered, comprising of 7,767 projectiles of which 838 were of toxic content.

The local population is often reluctant to plough previously unploughed fields due to disruption of the topsoil. Fields that are ploughed after several decades of 'rest' have a much greater risk from unexploded ammunition. Ploughing fields can result in lethal consequences in damage to both farmers and their machinery.

Australia sent 136,000 horses ('walers') overseas for use by the AIF during the Great War. Only the mount of Major General Sir William Bridges – 'Sandy' was to return. Transferred from Gallipoli to France via Alexandria, Sandy returned to Australia in November 1918.

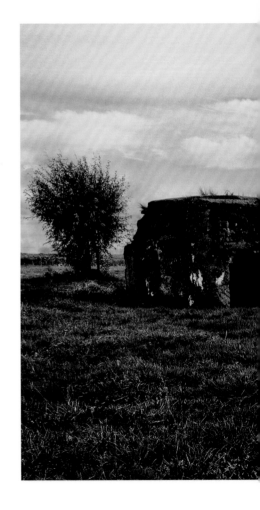

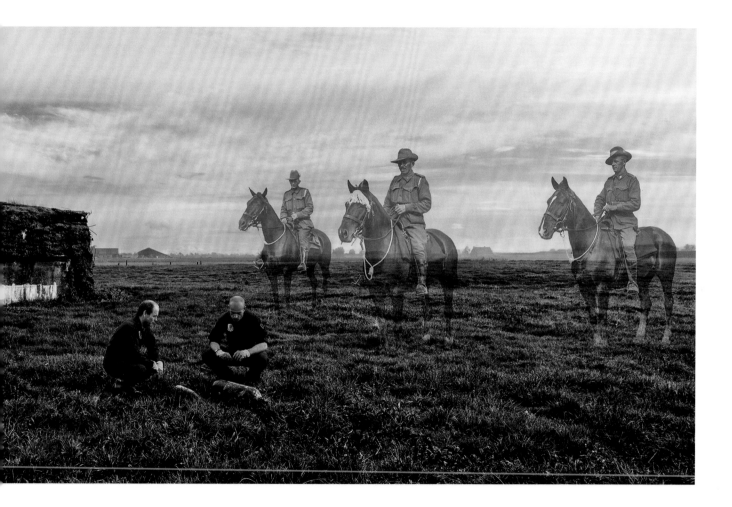

The unexploded ammunition will naturally rise through the ground over time, often assisted over the last few centimetres to the surface by the action of ploughing. A drive around the country roads of Flanders will invariably take you past unearthed live shells laid on the verges by farmers. In accordance with available human and material resources, these shells will be collected by DOVO-SEDEE as soon as possible.

The Australian soldiers in this image are taking observations using range-finding equipment.

The strategic advances made in battle were to prove only temporary, the psychological consequences of war on its men continued unabated.

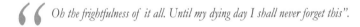

Oh the frightfulness of it all. Until my dying day I shall never forget this".

Captain Frank Hurley, official photographer of the AIF, 23 August 1917, Hill 60

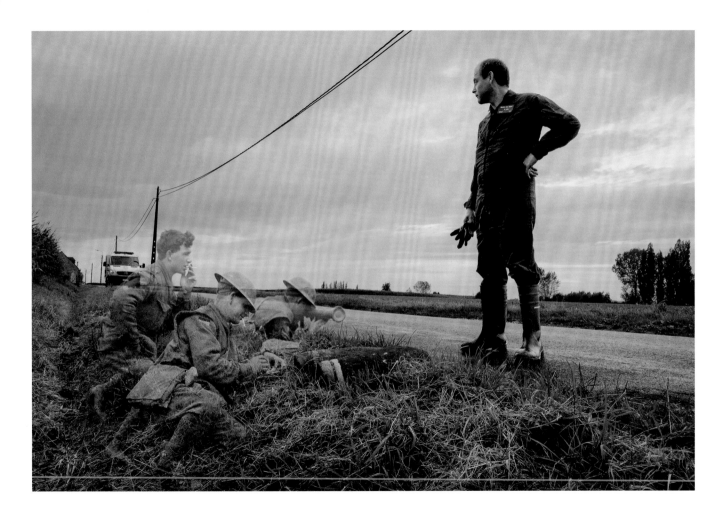

Unearthed by farm machinery whilst preparing the field for planting, a DOVO-SEDEE team recovers a hoard of 148 unfired French 7.5cm High-explosive shells.

A similar hoard was discovered the previous year just a few metres away suggesting that this was once a line of guns that were hurriedly moved to new positions, abandoning the ammunition in the process.

> *One of our men . . . went suddenly demented. The s.s [shell shock] had an electrifying effect on him . . . [He] dropped his rifle . . . rushed out over the front line trench into No mans land, the Germans blazing away at him: then he turned and ran down between the lines of the two armies; no one seemed able to bring him down. Then he turned again, raced into our own system, down overland through the support trenches . . . where men from the battalion pursued him, overpowered him, and forcibly rolled him in blankets and tied him up with rope . . . He was unwounded but evacuated raving mad."*

Capt R. A. Goldrick, MC, 33 Bn, of Parramata, NSW

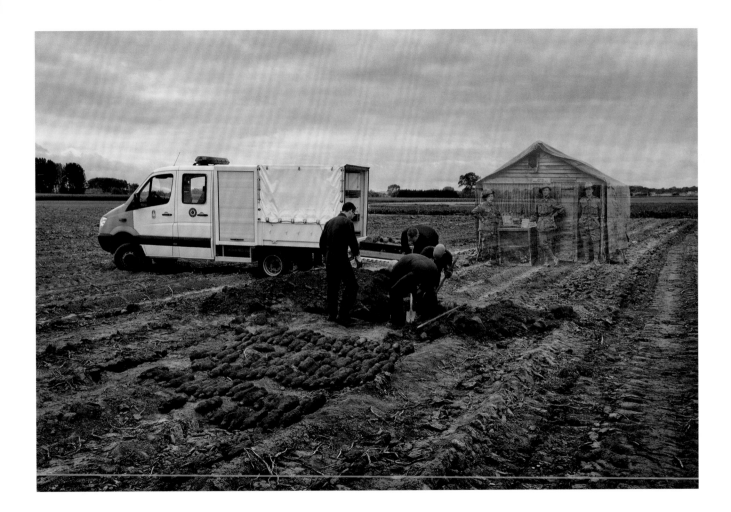

For security, farmers will occasionally recover unearthed ammunition to the safety of their farm until its collection by DOVO-SEDEE.

Toxic shells do not always contain gas but most of the time they will contain toxic fluids that turn into gas at the point of the shell's detonation. The leaking contents from corroding shells can result in catastrophic burns or blistering to the hands of those who choose to move them.

.

> " *[...] it all seems so horrible – and so unnecessary. I sometimes lie awake at nights, and think things over – and I often on such occasions pray that I shall not suffer from insomnia for a long time after the war . . . it would be too awful.*"

Lt C. V. McCulloch, 2nd Bn, Strathfield, NSW

Lt McCulloch was later killed in action aged 26, on 27 October 1917

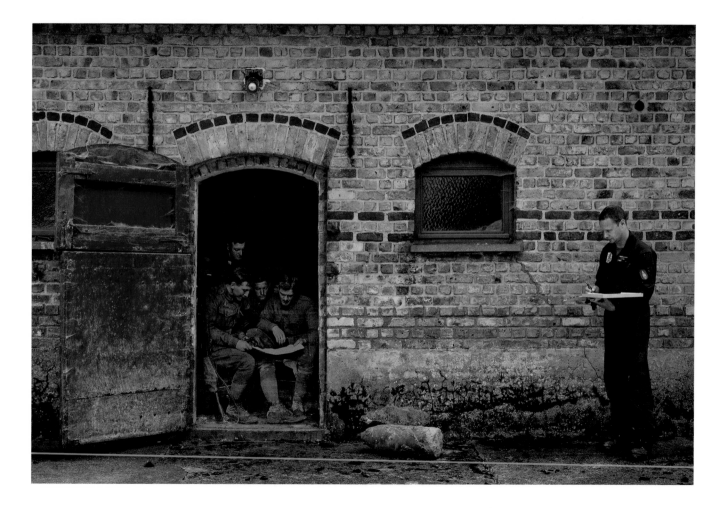

Shells containing a combination of both toxic (CLARK) and explosive contents are destroyed in a Contained Detonation Chamber (CDC). The CDC used by DOVO-SEDEE was the first such device in Europe.

The ammunition together with a donor charge is hung centrally in the chamber before the latter is wired to an electric detonator. The giant steel door is closed and a vacuum created within the chamber to eliminate the pressure wave resulting from the explosion.

The chamber's immense steel walls are 10cm thick and capable of withstanding the fragmentation of the exploding shells. The chemical residue from the explosion is high in arsenic and other toxic byproducts, necessitating that the plant's operators wear biochemical suits.

In time the inevitable emotional and psychological traumas caused by the Great War – once restricted to the servicemen at the front – began to manifest its carnage on Australian society.

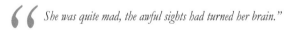 *She was quite mad, the awful sights had turned her brain."*

Matron Gertrude Moberly referring to an unnamed nurse of the
Australian Army Nursing Service (AANS)

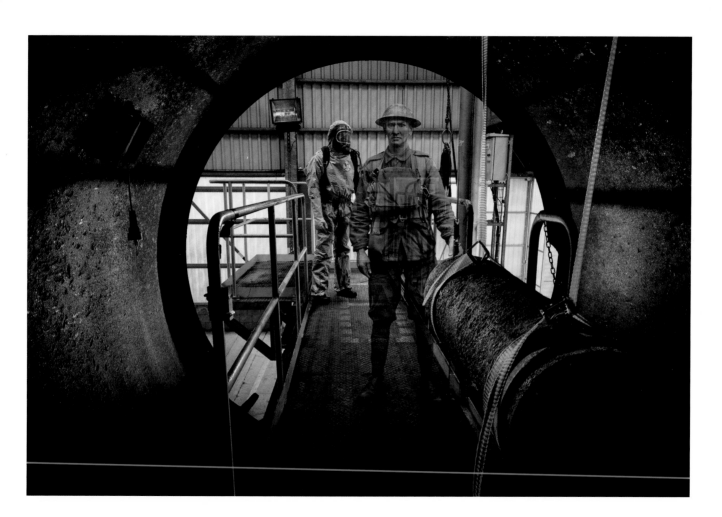

The local police who will have verified the shell's existence beforehand will give the unexploded ammunition's location, type and size to DOVO-SEDEE for its collection. The highest percentage of ammunition to be recovered will originate from farming and commercial development operations.

[...] we see some awful suffering from shell shock. One of the worst cases I have had so far is Lieutenant E-. [...] the nights spent with him were very tragic. [...] thinking he was asleep, when he would start up and scream out, "Oh God, the shells are coming" and turning to me would say "Quick lie down for your life! [...] and his voice would rise to a scream [...]. Oh the sadness of it all! I would hold his hand and soothe him [...]. This went on for nights."

Matron Gertrude Moberly, AANS

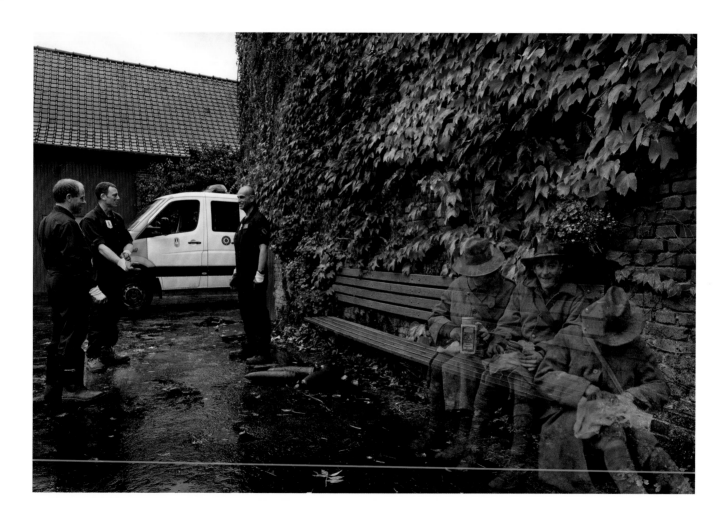

An 8in British High-explosive shell is recovered from drainage works being undertaken in the back garden of a house in modern day Passchendaele. For the residents of South West Flanders such finds are commonplace. The recovery of the shell to the awaiting truck is completed in a few short minutes.

In time the inevitable emotional and psychological traumas caused by the Great War – once the domain of the servicemen at the front – began to manifest its carnage on Australian society.

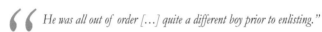 *He was all out of order […] quite a different boy prior to enlisting."*

Elsie Frank, speaking of her son Walter who returned home in 1918

.

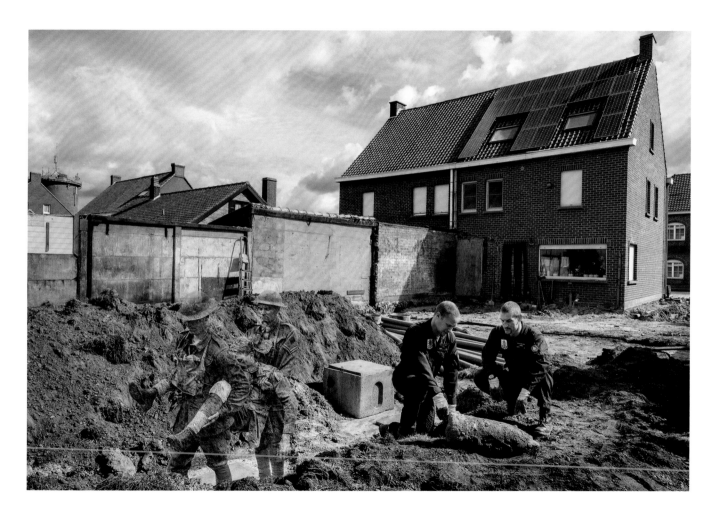

Two soldiers of the AIF are montaged into DOVO-SEDEE's ammunition reference section, the most complete of its kind in existence. At least one example of almost every shell type used on Belgian soil in this theatre of the Great War exists in this section of DOVO-SEDEE's Poelkapelle facility.

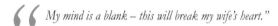 *My mind is a blank – this will break my wife's heart."*

Words on the note found with the revolver Evan Joseph Derby – of Canning Street, Melbourne – used to take his own life. Suffering from depression having been wounded and twice gassed in the war, Evan left a widow and four children.

Zeehan and Dundas Herald, Tas, Thursday 18 November 1920

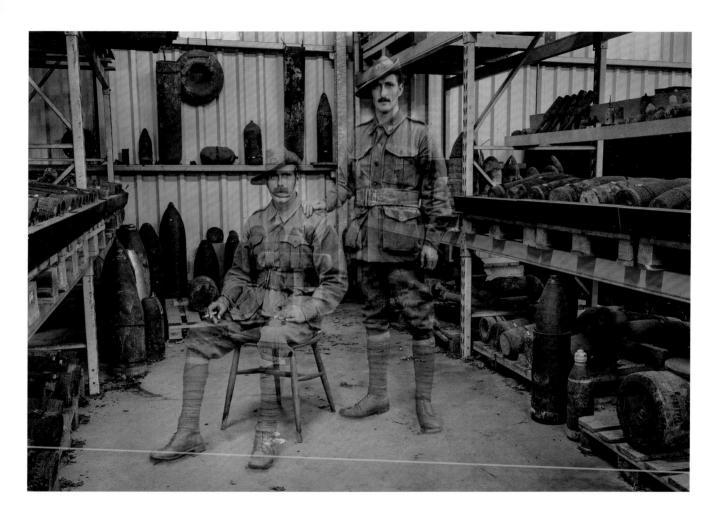

DOVO-SEDEE's Poelkapelle barracks can dispatch up to six separate teams of bomb disposal personnel per day to collect the enormous volumes of ammunition that continue to be unearthed from Flanders former battlefields of the Great War.

> *Daniel William Swadling, a returned soldier who was confined to his bed suffering from shell shock, committed suicide this afternoon by shooting himself with a pea rifle. As his wife walked into his room Swadling picked up a rifle which was near his bed, and saying "Goodbye", pulled the trigger. He died later in hospital."*

The Sydney Morning Herald, NSW, Thursday 2 May 1929

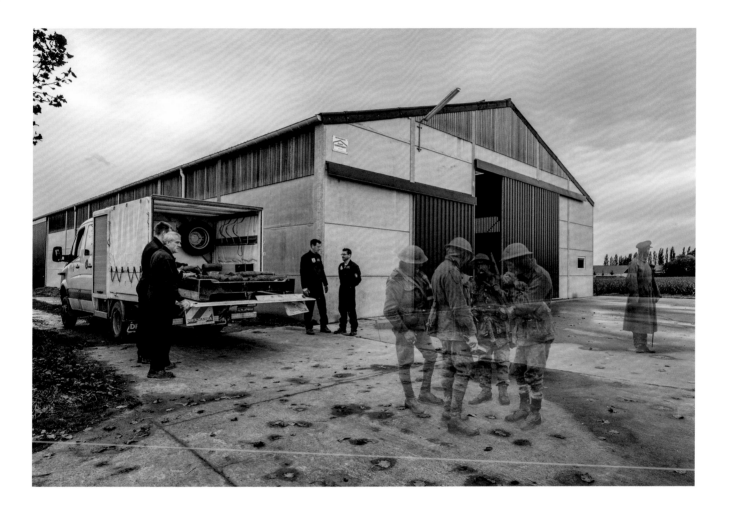

Two members of DOVO-SEDEE's carry unexploded ammunition from its point of recovery to their vehicle. Averaging circa 100 tonnes annually, twice a day from April through to October and under heavily controlled conditions, DOVO-SEDEE will bury and detonate conventional High-explosive ammunition recovered from in and around the former Ypres Salient.

> *An inquiry into the death of Charles Henry Delany, 42 years, laborer, of Hancock Street, Melbourne was held by the Deputy Coroner yesterday. Delaney was found dead at home on Friday night with a revolver bullet in his head. [...] Deceased was a returned soldier, was very "nervy" and suffered from shellshock. The revolver, which was found near the body, was one he had captured from the Germans."*

The Age, Melbourne, Thursday 5 October 1922

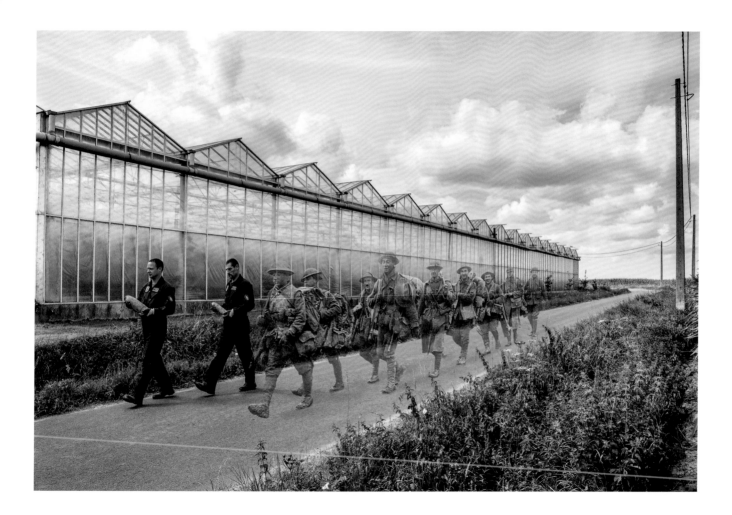

Flanders seemingly conventional flat landscape gives clues to its more sinister nature after periods of rain. As a result of a combination of a landscape destroyed through bombardment and prolonged periods of heavy rain, countless men and mules drowned in the morass at Passchendaele.

It took the population of Flanders three years of labour to fill the craters left after the fighting. During this time, exhumation companies – made up in many instances by the Chinese Labour Corps – worked tirelessly to exhume the fallen men from the then healing landscape.

The shooting of Mrs Anne, 61, near Wallan yesterday has caused a sensation […]. Frederick Curley, 22, who has seen much active service has been arrested. He has suffered from shell shock and has had fits of depression. […] He would wake up at night, calling out "The Germans are after me". He experienced terrible hallucinations."

The Grafton Argus and Clarence River General Adviser, Friday 17 February 1922

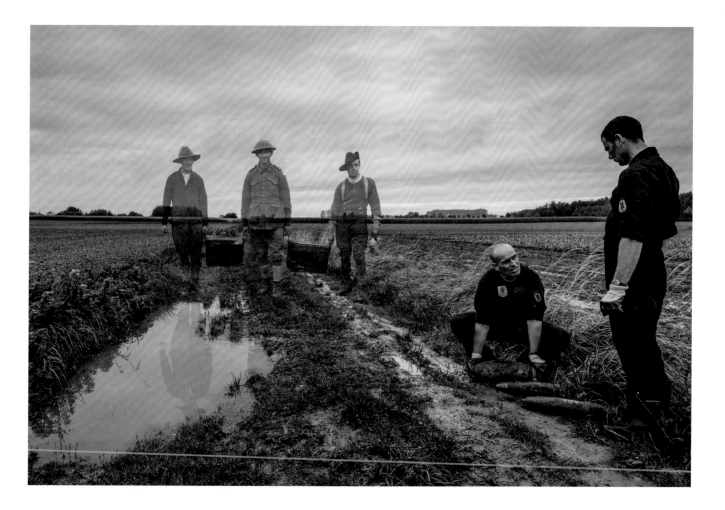

The landowner of this location has followed procedure and left the ammunition in-situ for DOVO-SEDEE to recover. Its specialist personnel are experts in all aspects of recovering and destroying the ammunition from Flanders.

" *All the horror and terror of war were revived so vividly in the mind of a returned soldier. M. Hibbard, of Brisbane, by a film in a Coraki theatre that he crumpled on the floor in a dead faint, showing all the symptoms of shell shock. […] he is slowly recovering but his memory has completely gone.*

Hibbard was a shell shock victim of the war, and collapsed when a vivid bombing scene was being portrayed. His muscles showed the agonized twitchings which were familiar to men at the front line during the war."

The Arndale Chronicle, NSW, Saturday 21 May 1927

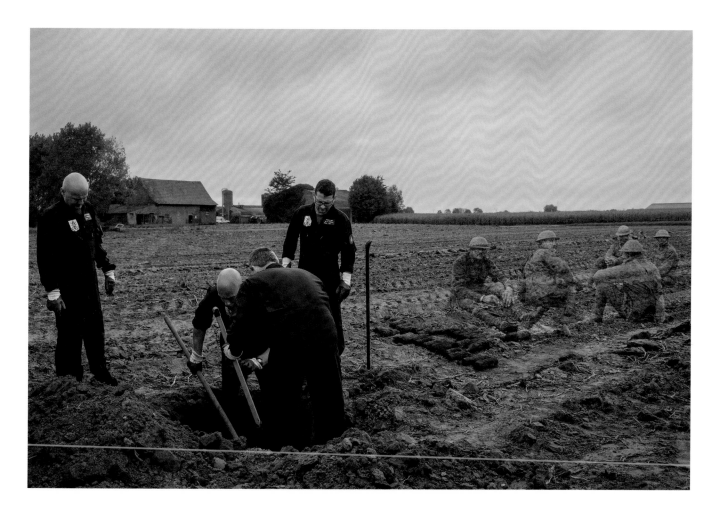

Belgium's explosive ordnance disposal service (EOD) was formed in 1920 and operated throughout the whole of Belgium. Similar operations continue unabated and on a much larger scale on the former Great War battlefields of France.

 The women of Australia gave their men to help our country, and us all, they paid the price then in months of anxiety and often in distress, and are still paying the price in suffering of the effects of war…"

Australian Red Cross Society, NSW, 1926

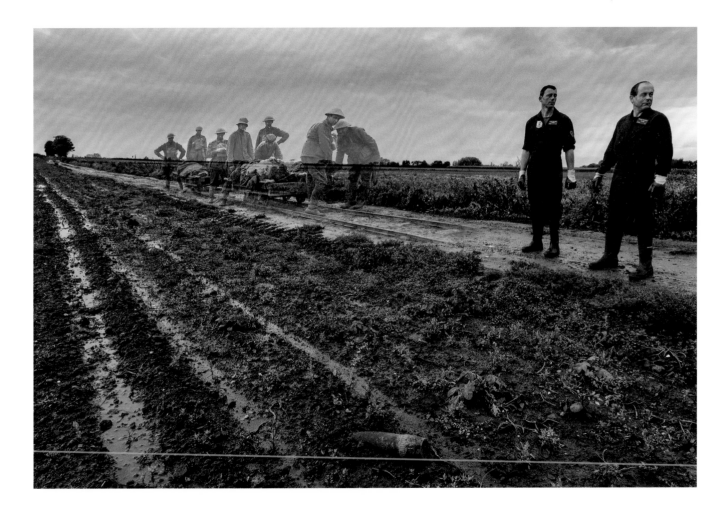

DOVO-SEDEE's activities are not restricted to land-based recovery of ammunition. Their specialised diving unit's work covers inland bodies of water as well as Belgium's territorial waters of the English Channel.

Mrs Lawrence had been an active member of the Rutherglen Red Cross throughout the war, but when her son returned severely wounded in 1918, she was unable to cope with the extent of his injuries [...] After returning her Red Cross identification card and collected donations, she 'went home and quietly took her own life.'

Bereft: War, Grief and Experiences of the Asylum, 1915–1935
Jennifer Roberts, University of Wollongong Thesis Collection

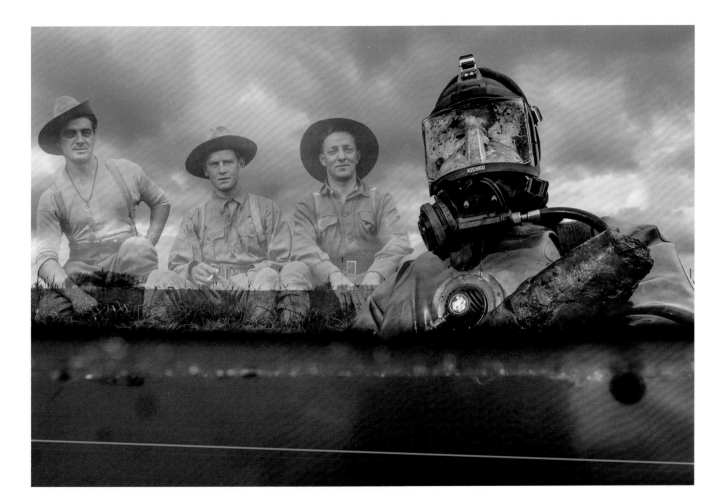

Recent shallow earthworks undertaken in preparation for the construction of a new commercial greenhouse near Poelkapelle resulted in the unearthing of eighty-five unexploded shells of various calibres and origin. In 2014, the removal of the grass from a meadow near Passchendaele revealed 820 shells of various calibres and contents.

In 1920, Julia Goulding of Brisbane, Queensland, wrote to the AIF headquarters in London –

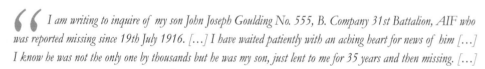

> *I am writing to inquire of my son John Joseph Goulding No. 555, B. Company 31st Battalion, AIF who was reported missing since 19th July 1916. […] I have waited patiently with an aching heart for news of him […] I know he was not the only one by thousands but he was my son, just lent to me for 35 years and then missing. […] The suspense is what makes it so hard."*

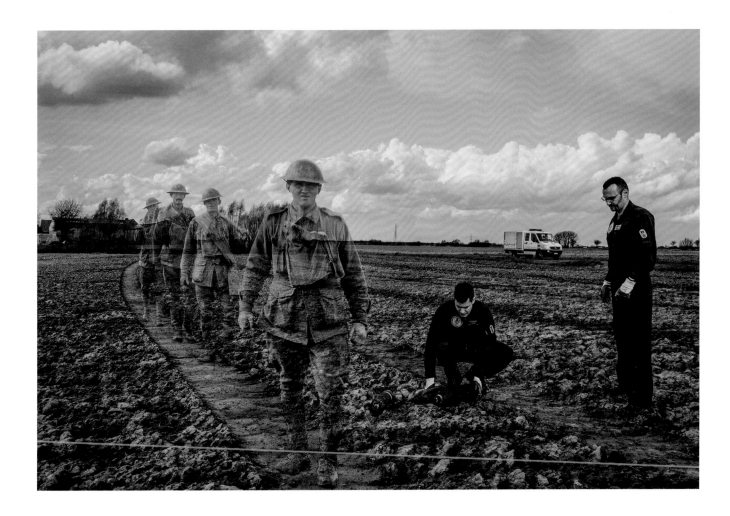

Through a largely unexplained process, the unexploded ammunition will rise slowly over time towards the surface. Owing to the farmers ploughing of the fields and the constant process of ammunition rising towards the surface, the Spring and Autumn ploughing seasons are the busiest periods for DOVO-SEDEE.

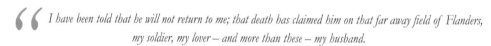

I have been told that he will not return to me; that death has claimed him on that far away field of Flanders, my soldier, my lover – and more than these – my husband.

And with the overwhelming shock came a numbness, a paralysis of all minor thoughts. One great fact occupied my mind day and night, burning itself into my very brain – "He is not coming back."

It all seems so impossible. […] It cannot be that the strong, handsome soldier who left me but a short year ago is cold and quiet, never to speak to me again. […] The numbness continues, and I realise nothing. […] His letters – cease to come. The numbness leaves me. I am awake to an all-prevailing fact. I am a war widow."

Excerpt from a letter entitled THE WAR WIDOW, and anonymously signed as ONE OF MANY *The Sydney Morning Herald*, **NSW, Wednesday 30 January 1918**

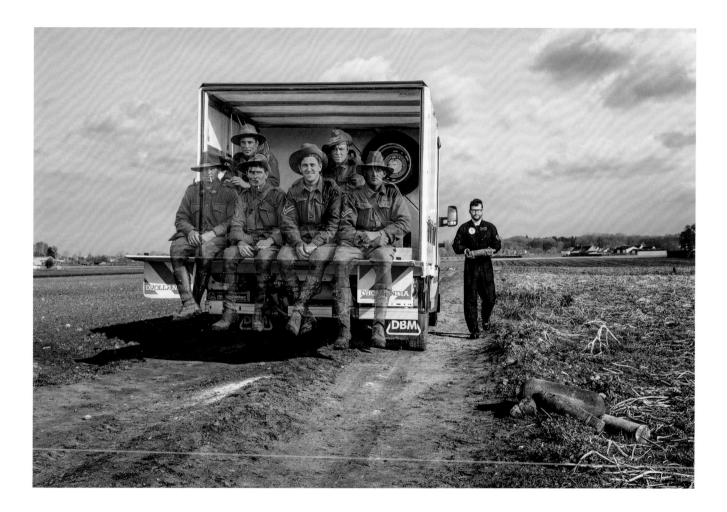

Two members of DOVO-SEDEE are pictured at the collection point where all recovered ammunition is brought for the purpose of identification.

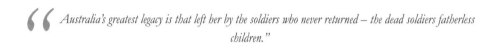

Australia's greatest legacy is that left her by the soldiers who never returned – the dead soldiers fatherless children."

Mr P. Board – chairman of the Soldiers Children's Education Board, August 1927

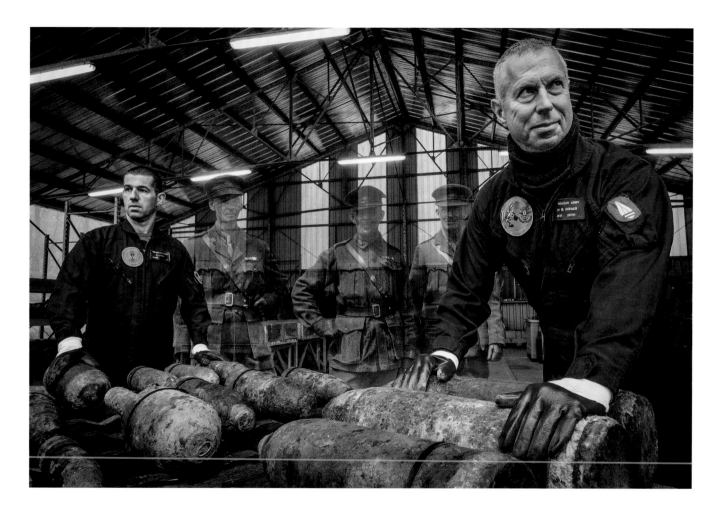

The term 'Iron Harvest' reflects the twice-yearly ploughing seasons whereby farming activities throughout Flanders former battlefields bring thousands of unexploded shells to the surface.

 When I go to bed at night, [...] if I allow myself to think of the war I'll get no sleep for the rest of the night, thinking of the things 'I should have done' and what 'I should not have done.'"

Dudley Jackson, 4 July 1967

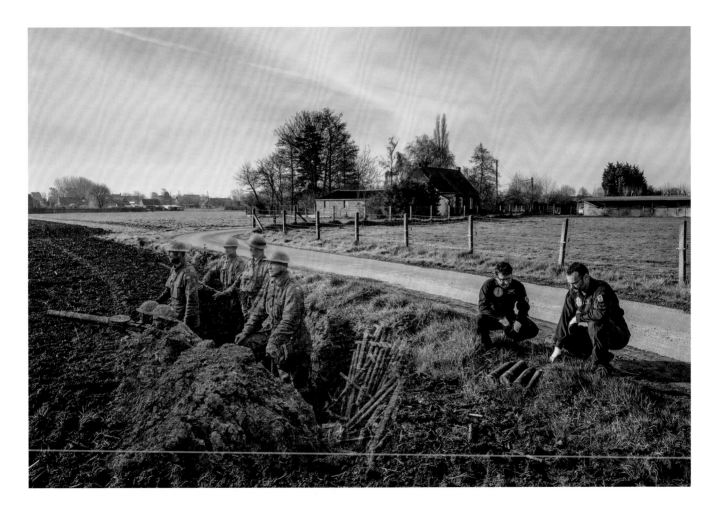

Each member of DOVO-SEDEE carries a tape measure. They are often able to identify the shell's origin from its specific measurements, external characteristics or fusing. The German Army used the diameter of a shell (such as 7.7cm or 15cm) to distinguish their ammunition. The British would use both weight and calibre, for example '15 pounder' and 8in.

 We thought we managed alright, kept the awful things out of our minds, but now I'm an old man and they come out from where I hid them. Every night."

Jim McPhee from Drouin, Victoria, a Field Ambulance veteran of Gallipoli and the Western Front

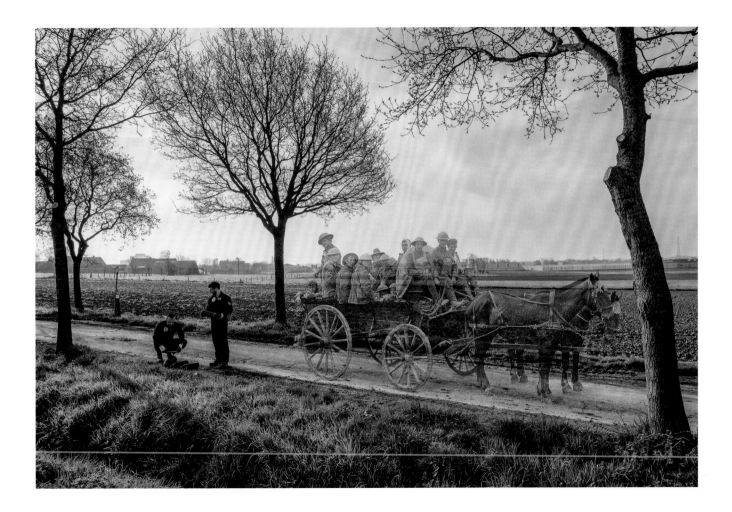

The final image of *Recovering The Past* sees the project's narrative reversed; as such it is a powerful statement of what lies ahead.

Unexploded ammunition and conflict-induced human trauma are not problems unique to the Great War, they apply to all wars since and those to come. All will leave a comparable tangible and lethal legacy for future generations to deal with.

Recovering The Past does not just enable its viewer to consider the troubling consequences of human conflict that this project explores, it stands as an opportunity on which they can be debated.

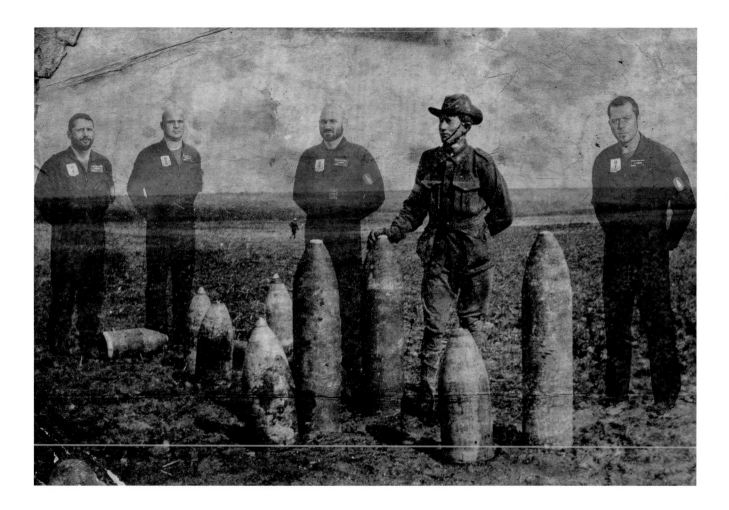

About the Artist

London based artist Ian Alderman has worked as a professional photographer for over 20 years. His passion for photography developed as a teenager through his desire to capture the drama of 'the great outdoors'. Extensive experience as both a photographer and digital artist has given Alderman the broad, practical knowledge required to produce a technically challenging project such as *Recovering The Past*.

Inspired by the brilliance and philosophy of photographers such as Frank Hurley, Henri Cartier Bresson, Margaret Bourke-White and O. Winston Link, Alderman's work continues to evolve, *Recovering The Past* is testament to this.

Alderman was allowed unprecedented access to photograph previously undocumented high-risk toxic environments for this project. The trust afforded to the artist by DOVO-SEDEE has enabled him to produce this unique study of the relentless and potentially lethal work of this major bomb disposal team on the Great War's former Western Front.

A complex project of over 6 years in the making, *Recovering The Past* has been produced with the centenary commemorations of the Great War and Armistice at its heart.

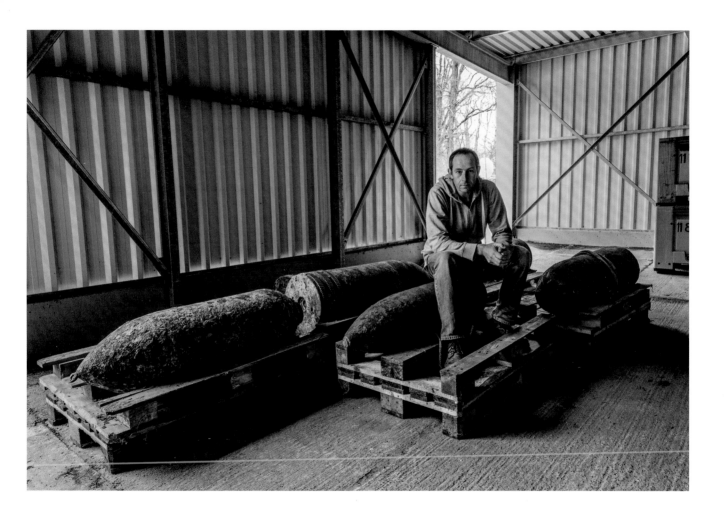

Limited edition prints are available of each of the images of *Recovering The Past*. Each individual print is supplied with a certificate of authenticity, and will be signed and numbered by the author.

For more information or to order prints please visit the website **www.recoveringthepast.com**